T0128271

Unleash YOUR Power

100 *Power* THOUGHTS BASED ON *Hello, Marvelous You*

JOCELYNE F. LAFRENIÈRE

BALBOA.PRESS

A DIVISION OF HAY HOUSE

Balboa Press books may be ordered through booksellers or by contacting:

Balboa Press
A Division of Hay House
1663 Liberty Drive
Bloomington, IN 47403
www.balboapress.com
1 (877) 407-4847

Print information available on the last page.

ISBN: 978-1-9822-3775-2 (sc)
ISBN: 978-1-9822-3777-6 (hc)
ISBN: 978-1-9822-3776-9 (e)

Library of Congress Control Number: 2019917301

Balboa Press rev. date: 10/24/2019

Contents

Acknowledgements

My loving thanks to my wonderful husband, Yvon, for believing in me and inspiring me to be all that I can be. Thank you for your support and encouragement. You brighten each day of my life with your love and joy.

Thank you to my close friends and family for your kind support. I truly cherish your friendships. A special thank you to my late mother, who raised me to pursue all my dreams.

My deepest thanks to Lee Ann from FirstEditing for her valuable editorial insights. Thank you to the Balboa Press team for their support and professionalism.

 *Dedication*

You were not created to be undiscovered and unfulfilled but to flourish, express your creativity and passion, and experience fulfillment with a sense of confidence, delight, and harmony.

You are endowed with freedom to create your best life. When your life lacks love, respect, confidence, passion, strength, and courage, it means you have forgotten—or were not aware—that you are the *Marvelous You*, thus drifting away from your true nature and shifting toward the *powerless you*.

This book is dedicated to all of you who choose to create their best life and be all that they can be. By choosing to activate our inner apps, we can realign ourselves and allow our true essence to rise from within and flow freely, thus replacing darkness with light in the world.

Start your day with reading a power thought. By nourishing your mind with these feel-good thoughts, you will cause your life to flourish for your own fulfillment and the betterment of others. You will unleash your inner power and actualize your *Marvelous Nature*.

Introduction

Let the seeds of greatness that are in you flourish to realize your *Marvelous Self*. Take a few moments each day to activate your apps. Your day ahead will surely be as you have never seen before.

Enthusiasm, inner joy, and harmony will be your faithful companions. With inspiration and intuition, you will move in the direction of your desires with passion and intensity. Love will shine through your eyes and embrace your words and behavior. In unity with God, you will awaken to a continuous sense of well-being, no matter what is going on around you.

As you go about your day, keep your apps activated. On occasion, we press the deactivation buttons and shift away from our *Marvelous Nature*. If you feel the strong pull of the *powerless you*, press the reset button and reactivate your apps. Let's have a look at how each of your apps empower your life.

With *True Inspiration* turned on, you light up the powerful creator that you are. Inspiration flows abundantly to help you become who you are meant to be. You master the ability to tune in to your intuition. Gone are limited beliefs and chaos in your mind.

High Drive puts little feet under your dreams by helping you craft a plan to bring action to your passions. With commitment, you move towards your vision. You unlock your full potential for the manifestation of fulfilling life experiences.

Managing your emotions is so much easier with *Dynamo*. This app alerts you when your emotional temperature is going down and you are moving away from your well-being zone. You can swiftly take action and bring more passion into your life.

With *Higher Power*, you ignite an interactive relationship with God. In oneness with him, your soul is enlightened. You experience acceptance, wholeness, and harmony. In this communion, bliss and praise are in your heart each day.

Be Happy fills your mind with feel-good thoughts. You speak words of possibility. You embrace a positive attitude. You live life with enthusiasm and passion. Your heart is grateful for life, today and tomorrow.

By turning on *Fit and Fab*, you automatically activate your membership to the *Fit and Feeling Fabulous Club*. You commit to nurturing and caring for yourself. You say yes to a life transformation with more fitness, vitality, and wellness.

With *Love Power*, you embody love, patience, forgiveness, kindness, and humility. You forgive your own faults, understanding that you are on a journey of growth.

Financial Tycoon helps you create financial growth in your life for your own pleasure and the benefit of others. You become a channel for richness to flow in the world.

Go-Getter helps you land your dream job. You are disciplined and well-organized. You are passionate about your work. You are a leader who does not shy away from responsibilities. You communicate positively and are well-respected by your peers.

With *Fly High*, you are a strategic thinker and successful entrepreneur. You welcome change to drive growth and improve performance. You strive for success. You create a culture of excellence, and are an inspiration to your team.

Fun and Play brings more leisure time into your life. You say goodbye to stress and say hello to more playtime, relaxation, and quietness to energize your body, ease your mind, and increase your well-being.

Green Thumb helps you declutter, complete the incompletes, transform your home into a comfortable refuge, and work area into an inspiring oasis. Home hygiene and economics are no longer a burden. You happily green your life.

With each of your apps well activated, you will discover your true self in all its beauty. In this inner transformation, you will experience the fullness of who you are, the *Marvelous You*. You will shine, and leave your footprint in making this world a better place.

Hello, Marvelous You

You are equipped for greatness.
Don't try to be great, just be great.

You are a spiritual being with a soul,
living a physical experience.

You hold the power to create your
best life.

A desire is an exciting vision of the
great opportunities that lie ahead.

Embracing change opens the door to
new possibilities.

You are the

Marvelous You,

born to create

your best life

 *Day 1*

It's your time to shine; seeds of greatness are in you.

Many people have wonderful aspirations for their future, but far too many do not pursue them. Unlike visionaries who are driven to create, grow, and expand, many are passive observers of life, waiting for change to materialize while putting in no effort.

Your true purpose is to actualize your *Marvelous Nature*. Don't be afraid of big dreams that speak of your greatness. You deserve to manifest the desires of your heart in synergy with God, who co-creates with you.

You want more for your life? Dream more. Love more. Serve more. Give more. More is what moves your life from good to very good. By seeing a new life in your mind, you will take the action needed for change to come. You are the spark that ignites change. Do not settle for less than you are. Resolve to become a better you. Dream from a place of abundance that reflects your true essence. Choose to be uncomfortable sometimes, outside of your comfort zone. Activate your faith and get ready to embrace your full potential.

Power Thought

*I dare to explore new horizons. I take steps in the
direction of my desires. I honor all that I am.*

Day 2

Follow your passion relentlessly; moments of doubt are not signs to quit.

Don't be turned off when you face obstacles and glitches. On the contrary, welcome them as experiences to fully actualize your *Marvelous Nature*. Challenges are springboards to achieve your full potential, and you are fully equipped to overcome them and live in victory.

With a positive attitude, challenges become opportunities to improve, advance, expand who you are, and enrich your life, not oppress it. By looking at obstacles in a different light, you are empowered with more vigor and passion to pursue your vision of success. Creativity abounds. Courage, resilience, and hopefulness become your constant companions.

Continue to move in the direction of your desires relentlessly, even when you face setbacks. If one plan fails, simply craft another one. There is no such thing as failure, only a better understanding of what works and what doesn't. From this state of positive expectations blossoms success.

Power Thought

I am fully equipped to embrace challenges. The power of courage and resilience is in me. With vigor and confidence, I keep my focus and continue to move toward my vision of success.

Day 3

When life leads you onto a dark road, let faith light up your path.

The Life Force that sustains the universe holds you in his hand. He has the power to transform the impossible into the possible. When you are walking on a road of unemployment, sickness, or broken relationships, activate your *Higher Power* app and light up your faith for courage and hopefulness to fill your heart. Soon you will see sickness giving place to health. Scarcity will make room for richness. Unhealthy relationships will be replaced by true companionships. Joy will dry your tears.

Faith gives you the power to move on and take action to better your life. It gives you the assurance that as a co-creator with God, everything will work out for the best. Faith fills your heart with joy and peace, knowing that great victories are on their way. You expect great things to happen. Without attachment to the outcome, you allow the universe to surprise you with more than expected. You keep your head up and rejoice in the waiting.

Faith keeps you excited for another day of possibilities. You look forward to new opportunities and experiences. You trust in the grander plan of life. You know that the journey is a thrilling adventure with new beginnings for your greatest transformation.

Power Thought

As a co-creator with God, I know deep in my heart that everything will work out for my best, even if it doesn't seem that way in the moment.

Day 4

Focus on what you want, not on what you do not want.

You are not defined by what your family or friends say of you; you are defined by what God says about who you are in his eyes. You are a wonderful being, worthy of his love and your love. You are precious in his sight and he delights in you. Richness is meant to flow in your life with talents, friends, love, happiness, and all good things.

If you don't like your life as it is now, challenge your thoughts and beliefs. Beliefs and thoughts must be congruent for manifestation. What you believe drives who you choose to be and what you create in your life. With your beliefs well-aligned with your aspirations, you are moving toward goal achievement at a faster pace. Nothing will stop you, not even an obstacle.

By focusing on what you do not want, however, you are drifting away from what you *do* want. If you do not believe you are worthy of all the riches God has in store for you, they will not come to pass. Take a few moments to reflect on beliefs about yourself that you need to reprogram.

Power Thought

I am marvelous in the eyes of God, deserving of abundance in all areas of my life. I choose to believe that I am worthy of his love and my love. Gone are limited beliefs and chaos in my mind. I take action for richness to flow in my life.

 *Day 5*

Bloom where you are.

Inner joy comes when you are grateful for who you are and where you are. Be proud of yourself. Be proud for all that you have accomplished so far. You do not need to compare yourself with others and feel threatened, superior, or inferior.

You are unique, with your own purpose. Appreciate the accomplishments and great beauty you see in others, but most importantly, be grateful for your own gifts. Be excited for today and tomorrow. Be a source of inspiration. With a positive attitude, you are a great testimony to who you truly are, the *Marvelous You*.

Bliss awaits you when you take action and await the outcome with detachment. When you voice your aspirations without attachment, you are open to different paths. You acknowledge that God co-creates with you. You have faith that he may surprise you with *hows* beyond your imagination. In this state of awareness, your heart is uplifted and full of praise for his awe-inspiring magnificence. Waiting moments are no longer moments of agony but moments of creativity, hope, courage, and inner joyousness.

Power Thought

I stand strong in faith, and I bloom and shine anywhere and anytime.

Day 6

Joyful expectation gives power to the manifestation process.

You are a powerful creator. With a single thought, you ignite the manifestation process. Through joyful expectation, your thought remains alive. And soon, you spread your wings to get into action.

Connected to God, the Life Force that sustains the universe, you recognize that he co-creates with you and orchestrates the fulfillment of your desires. It is faith that enables you to soar high to a place of greater success.

With your *Be Happy* app activated, your mind is filled with feel-good thoughts. You speak words of possibilities. You embrace a positive attitude. You live life with enthusiasm and passion. Your heart is grateful for life, today and tomorrow.

Dare to dream. Dare to heed the calling of your heart. Dare to rejoice. Dare to take action. Dare to expect in faith. Rejoice today for what is coming tomorrow. By keeping vibrational harmony in your thoughts, emotions, actions, and faith, you create magic in your life.

Power Thought

I choose feel-good thoughts that make me vibrate in harmony with my desires. I trust that God orchestrates my success. He inspires each of my steps as I move closer to my dreams.

Jocelyne F. Lafrenière

Day 7

Imagination is a powerful tool intended to create prosperity.

You are gifted with imagination to create new opportunities for your life. As you move toward your vision of success, you may encounter duality in your mind and emotions: confidence and fear, hopefulness and discouragement, glee and sorrow. To create your heartfelt aspirations with more ease, you need to master your mind and emotions.

Keeping your thoughts captive in positivity helps you remain in your well-being space, away from emotional distress. As you learn to use your imagination for its intended purpose of creating richness in your life, you will become better at attracting prosperity in all areas: physical, mental, spiritual, professional, family, social, and financial.

Feel-good thoughts plus action pave the way to success. Imagination is not meant to conceive self-sabotaging fears that lead to anxiety. Choose your thoughts wisely to keep the negativity monster at bay.

Power Thought

When plagued with negative thoughts and emotions, I swiftly let my mind dance with feel-good thoughts that bring about confidence, hopefulness, and glee.

 *Day 8*

Your mind is an animal that must be tamed.

By practicing *Flash Mob Thought*, positive thinking is made easy. The moment a negative thought comes to mind, all you have to do is swiftly respond with a *Flash Mob Thought*. Let your mind dance with feel-good thoughts that destroy barrier thoughts before they become powerful. Look at all you've accomplished so far; the new friendships you've developed, the new experiences that have come along. You see waiting as an opportunity to express courage, resilience, confidence, and be even more creative.

Focused, you happily press on and continue to march toward your vision. By getting into action, you create momentum and celebrate each of your efforts, job interviews, auditions, or business proposals. You are creative and open to new ideas. By keeping your mind on a tight leash you feel deep joy, peace, and gratitude, knowing that all will be well.

Power Thought

*I will not fall prey to distressful thoughts. I
choose to have a happy, positive day.*

Jocelyne F. Lafrenière

 *Day 9*

One who serves God each day keeps sadness and loneliness away.

Are sadness and loneliness lingering in your heart? If you have answered this question in the affirmative, then it's time to turn your life around and bring healing to your soul. You are uniquely gifted with talents, skills, and capabilities, and you hold the power to serve God each day and bring more wellness and grace into the world.

When you understand that you are the *Marvelous You* who co-creates with God a world of love, then sadness will be replaced with joy, and selfishness will be traded for selflessness. Your life will have a new meaning, and God's love will heal your wounds.

You will deeply feel wholeness, a sense of delight, and bliss in your soul, and your eyes will open to the beauty of your true essence. This will be the day of a new beginning for you.

Power Thought

*I am a being of love. I use my gifts and talents to honor
God, serve others, and create a better world. I wake up
each morning with excitement for what is to come.*

 *Day 10*

Harness all the possibilities that are within and around you.

No dream is ever too big. No dream is impossible. With every desire that is in your heart comes the drive and the will to bring it to light. Be daring! Dare to try! Dare to succeed! Success comes when you believe your best days are ahead of you, not behind you. Believing in the goodness of tomorrow gives you the power and momentum to create an awe-inspiring legacy.

You are gifted with talents, skills, and capacities to make a great contribution to this world. You alone hold the key that unlocks your full potential. To ignore your profound calling to live to the fullest is to say no to life and yes to the death of your soul.

Live to know all that you can be and do. Learn something new. Try something new. Each new step allows you to expand. With each victory comes more confidence.

Power Thought

I dare to expand and be more than I am today.
I trust in the goodness of tomorrow.

Jocelyne F. Lafrenière

 *Day 11*

Peace is the song of a loving heart.

You are the *Marvelous You* whose heart draws near to God, where you find deep-seated peace. Cultivate this peace to bring it to the world with kind words, forgiveness, and actions for the betterment of all.

You are a thoughtful companion, a caring parent, a skilled listener, a compassionate comforter, a patient teacher, a loving guide, a nurturing provider, and a peace activist who uplifts everyone around you. As you actualize your *Marvelous Nature*, you become fully aware of the grand scheme of life and you see how we are all connected in a sea of energy.

You embrace diversity and the power of differences. You have the utmost respect for different cultures, genders, races, and ethnicities. You want more for others and you are driven to create a new world where people of all religions and philosophies of life live harmoniously. You resolve conflicting perspectives with an understanding mind and open dialogue, using peaceful means. You strive for respect, compassion, and the well-being of all. Your song of peace disintegrates barriers and transforms the world.

Power Thought

I let the power of peace transform my life. With my heart captive in God's love, my lips sing a song of harmony. I honor diversity and pursue goodness.

Day 12

Be a prayer warrior and let God win your battles.

Earnest prayer and unwavering faith are the most powerful weapons to win many battles in life. God has the power to unbind what was bound, transform losses into gains, and move you to where you want to be in less time, using the most surprising ways. God can align events, circumstances, and people in your life like no one else. He has the power to speak through anyone's higher conscious mind and inspire you and others to do certain things, yet always respecting your free will.

In his great wisdom, God will give you a response that is in your best interest. If the answer is a long time coming, it may simply mean not now. If your desires are not aligned with his will, God will inspire a new prayer in your heart.

When you remain in a state of openness and trust, God will give you the grace to accept the answer. Don't be anxious in the waiting. God hears you and is at work. He takes care of all the details. Not seeing the fruits does not mean the seeds are not growing. Let the joy of stillness found in the crease of his hand fill your heart. Praise him for all the good that is coming your way, at the perfect time.

Power Thought

In all confidence, I come to you, O God, to offer my earnest prayers. I know you have the power to transform the impossible into the possible.

Jocelyne F. Lafrenière

 *Day 13*

When you raise your love vibration, not only do you find love, but love finds you.

Looking for more love in your life? Simply by raising your love vibration, you will become a magnet who will not only find love but will attract love. On occasion, loneliness, anger, criticism, chaos, or crisis deactivate our *Love Power* app. We shift away from our *Marvelous Nature*, and our love vibration weakens.

When you recognize the strong pull of the *powerless you*, press the reset button and reactivate your *Love Power* app. With your *Love Power* app activated, you live on the side of love. Your heart overflows with kindness, patience, understanding, and compassion. You choose to forgive those who have hurt you, and you cover their faults with love.

Each of your days should be a celebration of the love that is in you. And by opening to love, you will experience more joy and fulfillment from your relationships. You will attract more love and abundance in your life.

Power Thought

I let love fill my life with a new song. By living love,
I actualize my Marvelous Nature. I open myself to
receiving more love and abundance in my life.

 *Day 14*

Think Big!
Success is waiting for you.

Dare to be all that you can be and set goals that are challenging and will cause you to grow and improve. *Stretch goals* allow you to discover who you truly are, a being of expansion. They enable you to unleash the many truths of your *Marvelous Nature*, your own uniqueness, confidence, courage, and passion.

Stretch goals allow you to grow as a person, deepen your knowledge and skills, discover your gifts, tackle challenges, reach bigger goals, and learn perseverance, teamwork, quality work, and so much more.

Dare to dream bigger dreams. Surprise yourself with how much more you can do and be. Thinking defeated and limited beliefs will not move you in the direction of the dream that beckons you. By thinking big, you allow your mind to believe and create those larger-than-life dreams of yours. And with positive actions and faith, you engage in the manifestation process.

Power Thought

Hello, success! I am coming to you with passion and excitement. I let go of my limiting beliefs. I speak words of faith and victory. I take positive actions to move in the direction of my vision of success.

Jocelyne F. Lafrenière

 *Day 15*

You are the child of a King who makes wonders. No obstacle is too overwhelming.

Open your heart to God and let him know your worries, problems, and disappointments. He has the power to make wonders in your life. There is no need fearing tomorrow nor being anxious for what is to come; he will inspire you and guide your steps.

Hold your head up and keep walking in faith. God is going before you, and he will open the way on your behalf. He will fight your battles. Trust in him and have courage; no situation is hopeless for a child of the King.

With a grateful heart, thank God for all your blessings and what is to come. With faith comes the power of transforming the impossible into possible. Remember, it is during incomprehensible chaos that your eyes can see the power of the Great One.

Power Thought

I am a child of a King who makes wonders in my life. I am armed with trust, hope, and confidence. With my eyes on him, I fear not, nor am I anxious. My heart is filled with joy. He walks before me and fights my battles. With him on my side, I am a conqueror!

 *Day 16*

If you are not happy with your life, don't wait for change to come. Be bold and change it.

Each one of us has a unique purpose. When your unique purpose is not brought to fruition, your life will likely lack fulfillment, enthusiasm, satisfaction, and passion. If you long for change and you don't see it coming, be brave and create it. Excuses are not going to make things better. Don't settle for less in life; you deserve to live your passion.

Stop going around in circles and claim your full power by taking steps each day that move you in the direction of your desires. Don't delay any longer, waiting for your life to change. Be present in creating your life, leaving the past behind. Change what can be changed, and let go of what cannot be changed. Such an attitude will keep your soul from discouragement and give you energy to face life's challenges.

Remember, change requires effort, commitment, and perseverance. Pursue your desires relentlessly. The payoff is big: a life that is more enjoyable, and most importantly, a life that makes you feel fulfilled.

Power Thought

I choose to live my life purpose and craft a plan that will move me in the direction of my desires. I am excited for what is to come.

 *Day 17*

Action takes you closer to your vision of success.

There are days in life when you just feel like giving up. You say to yourself, "I've had enough; I've tried, and nothing is working." Don't let setbacks deflect you from your aspirations. Challenges are not signs to quit, but signs to persevere. Not seeing the mountaintop does not mean you are not close. Keep climbing; you may be closer to the top than you think.

No matter what life throws at you, you have the power to bounce back. Harness your creative energy to conceive positive outcomes, not defeat. Activate the power of your faith and speak words of trust and victory. Always let your mind be filled with feel-good thoughts.

Perseverance gives you the power to take another step forward. Champions know that you create your heartfelt aspirations with commitment, dedication, and self-discipline. Embrace patience and a positive attitude; they are your best allies in making the climb easier.

Power Thought

Disappointments will not stop me from climbing. Perseverance gives me the power to reach the top. I let patience and a positive attitude be my great allies. Oh, great mountain, I am coming to you!

Day 18

Fill up your morning cup with joy, gratitude, and love.

Each morning when you wake up, take a few moments to fill your heart with joy, gratitude, and love. Imagine yourself walking on a path that leads to a beautiful garden of well-being. Breathe slowly, simply relax, and feel the joy of being in that radiant place.

Let your heart be filled with appreciation. Be grateful for your family, friends, home, work, and blessings. Be grateful for the seeds of your *Marvelous Essence* that you have discovered through the process.

Feel God's unconditional love embracing you and filling your heart with self-love. In this quietness, hear his voice speaking to you and guiding you. Open your eyes slowly; you will see that bliss is now engraved in your heart. Moved by a spirit of gratefulness, you will be excited for today and tomorrow.

Power Thought

My heart is filled with joy, gratitude, and love. Every moment of my day is a celebration of life. Negativity has no power over me; bliss is engraved in my heart.

 *Day 19*

With your dreams in mind, move into action with confidence.

Like a caterpillar, all is there inside of you to become a butterfly. You are fully equipped to soar to new heights of success. Each aspect of the manifestation process—conceive, commit to action, and celebrate—involves all that you are.

By embracing your body, soul, and spirit connection, you will experience greater wellness, enabling the manifestation of your desires with more ease. With commitment and dedication, pursue your journey with excitement and passion. Let lessons learned be an opportunity for growth. Expect great things to happen. Let God guide your steps and surprise you with more than expected.

Empowered by good feelings and faith, be grateful for what is to come. With a joyful heart, celebrate your accomplishments, small and grand. Feel the pleasure of the manifestation of your desires.

Power Thought

I take ownership of my life, and let today be a turning point where I choose to manifest the life I want.

 *Day 20*

When you feel the pull of darkness, let your faith pull you back to your happy place.

If you navigate in tumultuous waters and feel your soul drifting away from your happy place, activate your *Higher Power* app and keep your eyes on God to avoid drowning in disappointment, fear, and depression.

With God as your Lighthouse, no challenges can take away your inner joy. He is your peace in the troubled sea. He will see that you come back to shore safely. He has the power to calm the storm.

With feel-good thoughts, wake up hope and excitement for what is to come. Fill your heart with gratefulness for all that you are and have. Know that you are not alone; you co-create with All-That-Is. He will make you strong in the face of high waves. He will take away your fears and work miracles to transform your life.

Power Thought

My faith is in God who has the power to work miracles in my life. He is my Lighthouse in times of darkness. I trust in full confidence that he will protect me and carry me back to safety.

 *Day 21*

Let today be a day of joy.

True abundance is in you, and it is God's desire that you experience it at all levels—physically, emotionally, intellectually, financially, and spiritually. Activate your *Be Happy* app and fill your heart with joy today because God's favor will show up. Look for his blessings in all those simple joys of life that come your way.

You are richly blessed with talents, friends, love, and all good things. Be grateful for all the pleasures and wonders of life. Be content and humble, conscious that your talents are true blessings.

Enjoy creating growth for your own pleasure and the betterment of all. Take some quiet time for yourself where you nourish your communion with God. Be ready to receive more—or something better—than expected.

Power Thought

My heart is filled with joy. I am grateful for all the richness that flows in my life for my own pleasure and the betterment of others. I thank God for his blessings today and tomorrow.

 *Day 22*

Like a palm tree, you may bow down during a storm, but you will rise up.

As you journey through your life, you may encounter hurricanes with heavy winds and severe rains that may cause you serious physical and emotional damage. Adversity, sickness, divorce, and the loss of a job or a loved one may bend you for a time, but these high winds will not break you.

You may bend when your employer lets you go. You may bend when you do not have enough money to pay your bills. You may bend when you become sick. You may bend when your projects fail. You may bend when your loved ones die. You may bend when your spouse leaves you for someone else. The good news is that your *Marvelous Nature* makes you hurricane-proof. You will rise above your challenges.

Power Thought

I can withstand life's setbacks, disappointments, and losses. Like a palm tree, I may bend but I will not be broken. I may be disappointed, but not desperate. I may be sad, but not hopeless.

 *Day 23*

Fear not; God is always with you.

Is your soul engulfed with fear, sadness, anguish, or grief? Keep your eyes on God, and soon you will say goodbye to those negative feelings and say hello to fulfillment, deep joy, and appreciation.

You are from God and in God. You are in continuous connectedness with him, whether you acknowledge it or not. In his love, you find self-esteem and worthiness. Under his wings, you learn, grow, and become who you are meant to be. In the stillness of your heart, you feel his power all around you. In his presence, you experience pure bliss and inner fulfillment.

With faith and feel-good thoughts, your whole being offers high vibrations. In that happy and vibrant energy space, there is no room for hopelessness, discouragement, frustration, resentment, or fear. True inner joy and peace abound and rejuvenate your body and mind, giving you the motivation to create your best life.

Power Thought

Goodbye fear and sadness, and hello, life! With my eyes on you, God, my heart is filled with deep joy and fulfillment. Praise is on my lips for your faithfulness.

 *Day 24*

One who believes can move beyond the impossible.

Faith gives you the confidence to discover the limits of the possible. It moves you to discover the abundant possibilities that each day brings. You fear not for today or tomorrow. You are not afraid to step out of your comfort zone. You know that the Life Force that sustains the universe holds you in his hand.

As the *Marvelous You,* you are pure creativity, greatly inspired, and enthusiastic for new opportunities in your life. With feel-good thoughts and focused actions, you create your heartfelt aspirations with commitment, self-control, and perseverance. Attuned to Infinite Wisdom, you are intuitive and directed with knowingness on the path of fulfillment.

Don't be shy to set bigger goals and take action to move beyond the impossible. You will never truly know all that you can be without taking a leap of faith. When you expand out of your comfort zone, you see yourself growing and deepening your skills, talents, and creativity. With expansion comes new discoveries, excitement, and satisfaction.

Power Thought

*I am excited at the thought of what my life could be. I resolve
to take a leap of faith and move beyond the impossible.
I am ready for more good to come into my life.*

Jocelyne F. Lafrenière

Day 25

In allowing yourself to become who you want to be, you find freedom.

Each moment is a moment of freedom and choice. Your mind is free to choose positive thoughts and create a purpose-driven life. Your heart is free to hope, love, and cultivate peace. Freedom is yours to listen to the voice of Spirit and actualize your *Marvelous Self* without limits.

There is no greater freedom than to allow yourself to become who you want to be. You are gifted with talents, skills, and abilities to add beauty to the universe. Don't hesitate to move towards your desires and discover your full potential. Know in confidence that not only has God placed aspirations in your heart, but he has given you the power to achieve them.

By following your heart, your life will be less about struggles and more about manifesting who you are meant to be and what you are meant to do. With soulful purpose you will be heading toward a path of passion and success. Your enthusiasm will inspire others to cause their lives to flourish.

Power Thought

I choose to honor my true purpose. With excitement, I follow my inner voice and take action to manifest who I want to be and what I am meant to do.

 *Day 26*

Like a diamond, let your inner light shine for all to see.

Richness flows in your life with talents, friends, love, and all good things. With your unique gifts, talents, passions, you are meant to play beautiful music in the orchestra of life.

Seeds of greatness are in you, and your task is to let those seeds flourish for more abundance in your life and the lives of others. In achieving more, you become more.

Don't wait any longer and activate your *High Drive* app to put little feet under your dreams. Choose to live your best life for more fulfillment and well-being. Life is truly yours to create with all that you are. Each day is an opportunity to let your inner light shine. In your own unique ways, you bring more beauty to the universe.

Power Thought

I am excited to be part of this grand universe and use my unique gifts, talents, and passions for the betterment of the world.

Jocelyne F. Lafrenière

 *Day 27*

You have a safe place under God's wings of love.

You are embraced by God's divine love, pure creativity, and infinite wisdom. Under his wings, you find joy and peace at the core of your being. In connection with him, you are in complete harmony,

Your fears, sadness, and disappointments disappear. You trust in the grander plan that he has for your life. You are no longer afraid of what tomorrow will bring. You are armed with courage, strength, and resilience, fully equipped to bounce back quickly from adversity. Your heart is filled with confidence, delight, and great expectations.

You are grateful for all the pleasures and wonders of life. You are content and humble, conscious that your talents are true blessings. You enjoy creating growth for your own pleasure and the betterment of all.

Power Thought

I thank God for all my blessings and what is to come. I believe
that he co-creates with me, and he will see that my life is a
testimony of his greatness. I am at peace under his wings.

 *Day 28*

A desire is an exciting vision of the possibilities for your life.

Whenever you have a desire in your heart, know that you have the will to turn it into reality. Take time to listen to your heart. Engage in a self-reflection of what you want to bring into your life. Let your imagination flow with creative ideas.

Awareness is the spark to the creation of your best life. Heartfelt aspirations are messengers of possibilities for your life. They are true expressions of who you can be. They make you feel alive and empowered. They are sparks that provide the energy in the morning to nudge you into action.

Actions are the little feet that give life to your aspirations. Positive expectations that your desires—or something better—will come to pass are your springboard as you journey. You gladly expect the unexpected, allowing God to surprise you with his greatness.

Power Thought

I am destined for greatness. I honor those aspirations and passions of mine. They are gifts for the greater good of all.

Day 29

Gratitude opens the door to happiness.

Gratitude is an expression of love. Being grateful for all the goodness in your life raises your vibrations of energy for more well-being. Practiced daily, gratitude brings about more positivity, confidence, and happiness, shifting you away from negative emotions amidst hardships. It brings more happiness into your heart. In conscious awareness of all that you are and have in life, glee blossoms and becomes your constant companion.

Be grateful for your talents, friends, love, and all good things. Be grateful for life, today and tomorrow. Be grateful for all your successes, small and grand, but most importantly, for all the little joys and smiles that each day brings. Be grateful for being able to help others.

Gratitude is a celebration of all the beautiful moments that enrich your life. Take time each day to celebrate life, and let your heart be rich in praise.

Power Thought

My life is filled with moments of joy that make my heart smile and expand with gratitude. I truly appreciate all that I have. I rejoice in this moment and for what is to come.

 *Day 30*

There is more than one road that can lead to your destination.

Sometimes life may appear unfair, and some events just can't be changed. A setback is not always a sign to quit. It can be an opportunity for growth, creativity, and improvement. Faced with dark plights, acceptance is the way to freedom. By letting your predominant thoughts be positive, you accept that everything is there for a reason. You see life with a brighter lens. You face challenges with more grace. You welcome life's surprises with more ease.

Reflect on what you have learned, what worked well and what did not, and explore other alternatives that can move you from where you are to where you want to be. Pay attention to how you feel about each possibility. Speak to people you trust, analyze your options, and then choose wisely.

Remember that there is more than one road that can lead you to your destination. If one plan fails, prepare another plan. If a door closes, open another door.

Power Thought

I am growing and learning. Setbacks are part of life's lessons, and I welcome them as great teachers. I open my mind and heart to new possibilities for my life.

Jocelyne F. Lafrenière

 *Day 31*

You heal past wounds with love, compassion, and forgiveness.

We all get bruises as we experience life; some more than others. Bruises can transform you into a powerless and resentful person who is angry toward others and life in general. Some people carry so much anger that it takes significant space in their inner self.

In true forgiveness, you allow others to have their own journey and lessons to learn. You open your heart to the positive aspects of their lives and see them with eyes of love. From this place of greater understanding your anger diffuses, your pain dissolves, and your wounds heal.

With forgiveness comes emotional freedom, restoration, and inner peace. As you set yourself free from the anger chains, you make room in your heart for hope and confidence. You leave the past behind and look to the future with excitement. Your heart is hopeful for all the good things tomorrow will bring.

Power Thought

I love myself with all my good and bad experiences. I embrace my pain with love, compassion, and gratitude. In true forgiveness, I let the pain fade away. I choose to move forward and leave the past behind.

 *Day 32*

Let yourself be sunshine in people's hearts.

You are the *Marvelous You*, a sunshine born to warm people's hearts. You are love in action and you radiate kindness, patience, forgiveness, and compassion. As you serve and nurture others, your rays of love shine with great beauty and bring more joy and peace into the world.

Kindness is the high note that our hearts sing. You are meant to be a channel for the power of love to flow in abundance from your heart to others. Don't be shy to thank or compliment someone. Words of wisdom and acts of kindness are powerful in working wonders in someone else's existence. You may alleviate their burdens and light a spark of hope and encouragement in their life.

Share the love, share the light. The world needs your rays of sunshine and great beauty.

Power Thought

My mission is to spread joy by sharing words of encouragement and acts of kindness. I am excited at the thought of radiating the love that is in me.

 *Day 33*

Small acts of kindness carry with them joy, hope, and love.

An act of kindness a day will keep you radiant and glowing. Kind gestures do not have to be expensive and take a lot of time to have great power. Small ones are just as powerful in transforming someone's day. They carry so much beauty. A compliment, an email, or a note are all declarations that you care.

Kindness is contagious. By spreading joy around you, you inspire others to do the same. In this abundance of love, you recognize that we are one, connected to each other and to the Life Power that sustains this beautiful and grand universe.

In creating a connection, you transcend individual boundaries and awaken to oneness with humanity. You see the good in others and appreciate their gifts and talents. Your life is enriched by the diversity of views and experiences.

Power Thought

I enjoy creating moments that make people feel special. I look forward to spreading joy today and make this adventure of giving one to remember.

 *Day 34*

Don't quit on your dreams; keep them alive with action.

Perhaps you have lost your job, or your husband, and you are overwhelmed by disappointments. You think that life was not rigged in your favor. Your dreams were shattered, and you don't want to dream anymore.

Dreams were given to you by the Creator for the manifestation of fulfilling life experiences. Inspired desires come with the power to actualize them. Don't let life pass you by. Take ownership and create an outstanding life with feel-good thoughts and disciplined actions.

Activate your *High Drive* app, and put little feet under your dreams by crafting a plan to bring action to your passions. Be willing to take a risk. With commitment, move toward your vision. Surprise yourself with how much more you can do and be. Let your faith inspire you to believe in the impossible and remain in a state of positive expectation.

Power Thought

I am the co-creator of my life and I honor my unique purpose. With feel-good thoughts and committed actions, I move forward in the direction of my dreams.

 *Day 35*

Perseverance is what moves you to where you want to be.

A bad day today is not the premise for a bad day tomorrow. You are fully equipped to tackle challenges. Do not let a setback stop you from moving forward. Choose a different direction, keep walking, and go all the way to your destination. Failure does not exist, as life is all about learning what works and what doesn't. Growth stems from experiencing life to its fullest, with all its ups and downs.

Remember, God will guide you to victory. Faith is your powerful armor that keeps you strong. He co-creates with you. In his time, he will open the way for your deep aspirations to actualize and for your life to be a blessing to others.

Success is in you; success *is* you. Learn, dare, make positive, life-changing choices, and persevere. Without any doubt, your life will be a testimony of the greatness that is in you.

Power Thought

I take steps to move in the direction of my aspirations. I say no to opportunities that do not truly align with the direction I am heading. I remain consistent and persevere in my journey.

 *Day 36*

As you spread love around you, you become a love magnet.

When you express love and kindness, you animate the divine force that is in you. A legacy of love develops with each of your smiles, uplifting words, and kind acts of love.

Love is a helping hand. Love is taking time out of your schedule for someone in need. Love is a call to say I love you. Love is a little surprise to cheer someone. Love is listening. Love is being open to the ideas of others. Love is being patient. Love is respecting others. Love is giving back with a smiling heart. Love is supporting others in their efforts to become all that they can be.

A legacy of love also means respecting differences. Diversity is what makes us stronger. It enriches our lives and expands our view of the world. Being respectful does not mean you always agree; it means you allow others to be. Let love be your signature.

Power Thought

I create a legacy of love and gratitude. I cultivate goodness and forgiveness. By spreading love around, I am a love magnet.

Jocelyne F. Lafrenière

Day 37

Ask yourself what you can do today to enjoy life.
Soon, your life will be filled with magical moments.

Are you feeling exhausted, out of balance, or bored right now? Are you tired of waking up with no energy? It might well be because you suffer from the *Go, Go, Go Syndrome* caused by your fast-paced lifestyle and never-ending professional and family commitments.

Juggling our professional and personal life has become a real struggle. For many, life is filled with less and less leisure time, leaving their body and mind taxed and feeling totally depleted. Our bodies are not meant to constantly be in action. Activate your *Fun and Play* app for more time to downshift, relax, replenish, and enjoy life's pleasures. Self-care will bring joy to your heart and make you feel alive.

With less mind and body stress, your body becomes stronger, your mind is more alert, and you experience feel-good emotions. You deepen your connection with yourself, other human beings, and God, which in turn allows you to enjoy more well-being and appreciate life in all its beauty. The path to wellness is simple: nurture your body, refresh your soul, and heighten your spirit.

Power Thought

From now on, I say goodbye to my hectic schedule and I say
hello to more playtime, relaxation, and quietness to energize
my body, ease my mind, and experience more well-being.

 *Day 38*

Even in the darkest moments, when the rain falls on your life, know that a rainbow is waiting for you.

You are a wonderful being, cared for and loved by God. Have faith in his infinite power, and know his blessings and alliance are with you always during the good and bad times, like a rainbow after the rain. In him, you never feel alone. You are alive, with your heart and mind being fed by the seeds of his love. Inner joy and peace are with you each day.

Trusting in God creates the highest vibrations of energy, which in turn gives you more ease and confidence to tackle life's uncertainties and disappointing events. When you nurture your relationship with him, new beliefs and inner joy and peace take root in your heart. Your mind shifts to more feel-good thoughts, which in turn create positive emotions that move you into action.

Even if strong winds are blowing in your professional and personal lives, know that the hurricane season does not last forever. Keep an open heart, learn and grow, and stay strong in the hope of a better tomorrow while moving forward.

Power Thought

In God's hands, I take refuge where peace awaits me. I know deep in my heart that like a rainbow after the rain, his love supports me. All I need to accomplish my life purpose is coming my way.

Jocelyne F. Lafrenière

 *Day 39*

At times, your worst enemy is your mind. Positive thoughts keep you in your well-being zone.

Are you caught up in negative thinking patterns? With self-defeating thoughts come negative feelings, stress, and anxiety. You feel desperate. You are not inspired. You do not dare to dream of a better tomorrow. You do not take action.

If you want a shift in your feelings and are looking for change in your life, then you need to banish negative thinking. You have the choice to not linger on negative thoughts.

Be wise and recognize when negative thoughts come to mind. Heighten your well-being by responding quickly with positive thoughts that elevate your mood and release tension. By mastering your thoughts, you will move to the high zone of the emotion spectrum where you experience inner joy, peace, hope, and enthusiasm.

Power Thought

I am the guardian of my thoughts. I replace each negative thought with a feel-good one that elevates me to new heights of well-being.

 *Day 40*

When the journey ahead seems difficult, remember that each step takes you closer to your destination.

Plagued with moments of doubt? It might be time for you to realign your beliefs with your desires. Empower yourself with feel-good thoughts that move you in a high-vibration energy space and keep you flying high.

Do not get bitter or discouraged if you face obstacles or if things don't happen as planned. What looks like an obstacle may be an opportunity to grow. Stay strong and motivated. You are fully equipped to cope with and handle life's surprises. As you journey, assess your progress and reevaluate your strategy for the best results. Celebrate mini-successes and rejoice for having the courage to move in the direction of your dreams.

A delay does not mean a denial. Choose to be positive and move forward. You co-create with the Highest Power of the universe. In stillness, listen to his voice, as he will guide your next steps. God's plan is always the best.

Power Thought

I know that the Highest Power of the universe will open doors when the time is right. For this, my heart sings a song of peace.

Jocelyne F. Lafrenière

 *Day 41*

Let the force of love that is in you transform the world into a place of abundance and peace.

You are richly blessed, born to be a nurturer who never ceases to love and care for others. When you let love bloom around you, not only do you transform your life, but you transform the lives of others with more joy, hope, and peace.

Love nourishes the soul of those who receive it. It gives life and warmth, and it comes with beautiful moments that live on in our hearts forever.

Love embodies patience, forgiveness, kindness, and humility. Activate your *Love Power* app, and transform the world with a smile, kind actions, and wisely spoken words. From that place where true love flows, you see the world as your home and mankind as your brethren. Love is the best symphony that you can play in with people from all ethnicities, cultures, and religions.

Power Thought

I plant seeds of love—patience, goodness, and forgiveness.
As I choose to live love with an open heart, I bring more joy,
hope, and peace into my life and the lives of others.

 *Day 42*

Fear hinders you from moving toward your dreams. Free yourself from this burdensome restraint.

While fear may be a valid signal alerting you of imminent danger, oftentimes it is a creation of your mind. Fear is a prison, and doubt, worries, and negative emotions are your shackles. You cannot create your best life without breaking these chains.

You can free yourself from this dark prison and clear your mind of chaos and turmoil by replacing self-defeating thoughts and beliefs with feel-good ones. You have the armor to conquer your fears.

In remembering that you are in continual connection with God, you will become fearless, courageous, and engaged. You will discover empowerment and freedom. In oneness with God, you will be able to move toward your dreams with confidence. You are not meant to be a prisoner of fear, only a prisoner of God's love.

Power Thought

I am confident and hopeful for the abundant possibilities that each day brings. I fear not for tomorrow. I know that the Life Force that sustains the universe holds me in his hands.

Jocelyne F. Lafrenière

 *Day 43*

Believe, and open your heart to the impossible.

Imagine what your life would be if you would believe the impossible is achievable. You would dream again and set bigger goals for your life. Your heart would sing a new song, and each day would feel like a new adventure.

By harnessing the Highest Power of the universe in faith, you transform your life. You set yourself up to seeing the impossible become possible. Your thoughts are empowered, and you know deep in your heart that you can do so much more than what you are and what you have done today and yesterday.

Let hope fill your heart. Let God work with you and direct your steps. Allow his goodness to lift you up and give you the courage to be nudged into action. Let obstacles be a door for something greater. He has the power to open closed doors and do the impossible for you. Be at peace; God is working on your behalf.

Power Thought

I let faith transform my life. I let the Highest Power of the universe guide my steps. I am directed in life with divine inspiration and intuition.

 *Day 44*

To give up is not part of successful people's vocabulary, but perseverance is.

If your project failed, look for lessons learned and how you could do things differently. Look for a coach and mentors who can guide you in your next steps. Be inspired by what others are doing well and learn from them. Try again, but differently; do not give up, especially if your goal still lights up your heart with excitement and passion.

Embrace a positive attitude and let perseverance and patience be your allies. Read positive affirmations about your true nature. Empower your wants by practicing visualization. Let you heart be filled with joy for all the blessings coming your way.

Most importantly, know that all experiences, good and bad, prepare you for what is to come. Oftentimes, a door closes for something better to come into your life. Moved by a spirit of gratefulness, focus on what you have, not on what you do not have. Let yourself be excited by what is to come.

Power Thought

My future holds many more moments of happiness. I trust that God will bring into my life all that I need to live my true purpose.

Day 45

To rise above your limits, you must think big and set high goals.

Get ready to shake off your negative and limitless thoughts and rise up! It's time for your best life to flourish and for you to become the best that you can be. Get excited about living your aspirations.

Start by taking time to assess your personal strengths and weaknesses in each area of your life. Then, set stretch goals that allow you to discover your full potential. Dare to dream bigger dreams.

Inspiring goals aligned with your life purpose will drive positive actions in the direction of your wants. Not only will you transform your life, but you will bring betterment into the lives of others. As a result, your goals will keep you excited and engaged. Everything is possible to those who believe in the impossible.

Power Thought

I dare to dream bigger dreams; I dare to try. I dare to succeed. I celebrate my victories, small and grand.

Day 46

Set your sails in the right direction and move toward your aspirations.

You are who you are and where you are because you have created it with your thoughts and actions. No one coerced you; you chose it all. If you don't like what you see, step out of your pity party, stop blaming and complaining to those around you, and take positive action.

Who do you want to be: a visionary or a passive observer of life? Accepting responsibility for where you are today is the first step in a true transformation. When ready, you will bring to life the powerful creator that you are. Inspiration and intuition will flow abundantly, and your heart will be filled with desires that create a chain reaction that will turn them into reality.

You will then engage in crafting an action plan to nudge you toward a new destination. Embraced by good feelings and faith, you will be grateful for what is to come, yet detached from the outcomes. Don't wait any longer to let the world see that you are the *Marvelous You*, a powerful creator destined for greatness.

Power Thought

I take full responsibility for my life. I create change and turn things around. I am ready to fly higher in a space where inner joyousness resides.

 *Day 47*

Anger and sarcasm are the enemies of love.

In the heat of a debate, many choose harsh words as their weapon of choice to speak up about their frustrations. Unfortunately, sarcasm, coarse language, and shouting do nothing to resolve differences. Throwing poisonous words that kill love will only keep you in troubled waters.

Communicating in a calm and non-threatening manner will lead to a collaborative dialogue and a more fruitful outcome. When you're ready to leave your anger at the door, find a quiet place with no distractions to hash out the issue. Take turns in expressing your individual concerns and feelings. Work together in identifying an arrangement that is realistic and suitable for both of you.

Most importantly, ask for forgiveness, especially if you lost your temper and your words were abrasive. Forgiveness breaks barriers and opens the door to a loving resolution.

Power Thought

In the middle of a relationship storm, I remain calm. I keep my heart open to what is said and needed. With kind words, I choose to find a peaceful resolution, agreeable to both of us.

 *Day 48*

Do what is possible, and God will take care of the impossible.

Faith in the power of God is your most precious ally in life. It gets you to fly high and see the invisible. It gives you wings to soar to new heights. Faith reminds you that you are not alone; God is always there for you.

Faith empowers you to continue to climb even when you do not see the mountaintop. Your mind is filled with feel-good thoughts. You speak words of possibilities. You embrace a positive attitude as you climb with enthusiasm and passion.

Faith gives you courage and hope. Your heart is at peace, knowing that everything you need to succeed is in you. You expect great things in your life, and nothing less.

Faith keeps you strong. You climb up relentlessly, with confidence that God has the power to orchestrate events, circumstances, and people for your desires to come true at the right time.

Power Thought

I am confident about tomorrow because I trust in the orchestrating Power of Life. In him, I've found a place of inner peace. I know that all will be well and good.

 *Day 49*

By staying in your well-being zone, you fill your tomorrows with joy.

If your mind is pulling you toward dark thoughts, you need to turn on your *Be Happy* app to swiftly move back to your well-being zone where you offer high vibrations of energy. With *Be Happy*, everything about you and your life is enlightened with positivity. Joy is in the air.

You let go of past negative events and move through life's disappointments with more ease. You nourish your mind with thoughts of hope, abundance, and success. You are fired up and believe in your desires. You feel alive and ready to be the success you are meant to be. You allow intuition and inspiration to guide you. You are ready to live your best life.

You cultivate life mindfulness, where your eyes see the beauty in each moment. All the simple pleasures of life make your heart expand in gratitude. You raise your vibrations and move to your well-being zone where you find peace about who you are and why you are here.

Power Thought

With my Be Happy app well-activated, my heart is filled with inner joy.

 *Day 50*

One who masters his or her emotions has found the secret to inner bliss.

Emotions are like a roller coaster ride with speed, loops, and turns. Exhilaration and excitement when going up, fear and screams when going down. Positive emotions such as love, glee, confidence, appreciation, and enthusiasm make your eyes shine and radiate. They excite you for tomorrow. On the flip side, negative emotions like grief, depression, fear, hate, anger, disappointment, and pessimism make you wish there was no tomorrow. Under their spell, you are drifting away from your *Marvelous Nature.*

Activate your *Dynamo* app, which alerts you when your emotional temperature is going down. If you see yourself shifting away from your well-being zone, activate your faith, which in turn will bring about joy, hope, and trust in your heart.

Take deep breaths. By inhaling and exhaling, you invite glee and peace into your heart and you let go of toxic emotions and energies. Fill your mind with feel-good thoughts that will help you stay in a state of confident expectation for what is to come.

Power Thought

I choose to control unwanted emotions, not let them control my life. God is working on my behalf. I let glee and peace engulf my heart and I let go of toxic emotions and energies. With feel-good thoughts, I move back to my well-being zone.

Jocelyne F. Lafrenière

 *Day 51*

With love as your clothing, your heart is kept warm.

With *Love Power*, you enable your most important relationship, the one you have with yourself. You heal past wounds and crush the disempowering beliefs of being unworthy and unloved. You embrace your uniqueness, with all your strengths and weaknesses.

As a being of love you are a companion, a listener, a comforter, a teacher, a guide, and a provider who uplifts everyone around you. You embrace high ethical values.

Love is manifested in different ways. You are generosity when you lend a helping hand in times of need. You are compassion when you listen to someone else's pain. You are peace when you speak words of encouragement. You are a nurturer when you are kind to others.

Living love reminds you of your connectedness to God, who is the Source of true love. It brings purpose to your life, which in turn keeps your heart warm and full of joy.

Power Thought

I embrace my true purpose, which is to manifest love for myself and others. Kindness, compassion, patience, and forgiveness are my daily companions.

Day 52

Let God lift the heaviness that weighs on your heart.

Is sadness lingering in your soul? Do you feel lonely, wondering why you were put on Earth in the first place? Let me remind you that you are the *Marvelous You*. You were uniquely designed with creativity, personality, talents, skills, and capacities to add more beauty to the world.

Be hopeful for tomorrow and excited for the abundant possibilities that each day brings, even when your life suggests otherwise. In oneness with God, embrace with love who you are. In awareness of his presence, let your conscious mind be filled with feel-good thoughts. Know with assurance that God has the power to turn the impossible to possible. Let faith crush heaviness in your heart and replace it with inner joyousness, calmness, and gratitude.

Look for others ready to help you. Let people around you know how you feel. Talk to someone—a friend, a physician, a parent, a school counselor, or a support group. Know that emotional pain and suffering will subside. Having been wounded, you need time to heal. Get involved in the community. Meet people and happily serve others. As you love and receive love from others, your heart will heal.

Power Thought

I am a marvelous being created to bring more beauty into the world. With God as my Source, I can bring to life the seeds of greatness that are placed in me.

Jocelyne F. Lafrenière

 *Day 53*

If your life doesn't bring you happiness, then bring happiness to your life.

As a marvelous being, happiness is your pursuit. There are so many ways you can create happiness for yourself and those around you. Send a gratitude email or a card to someone you appreciate. Say thank you for a helping hand, or I love you to your loved ones. In doing so, blissful joy will color your soul like a rainbow.

Learn to celebrate yourself and the small joys of life. Become your greatest companion and create moments of happiness. Read inspiring books, prepare your favorite dish, listen to good music, go for a bike ride or a short drive around.

By keeping your conscious mind busy with feel-good thoughts, you give wings to your life to soar to a place of glee. With your faith activated, you are not troubled by rainy days; you have happiness and experience inner joy.

Let gratitude bring happiness to your life. Each moment is a moment to rejoice. By creating simple magic moments during your day, you keep your soul and spirit in a high-vibration energy space where well-being resides.

Power Thought

I create magic moments that bring happiness to myself and those around me. I am grateful for the simple joys of life.

 *Day 54*

Trust in the power of God to guide your steps each and every day.

When you soar to a higher level of consciousness and choose to replace limited beliefs with a vision of new possibilities, you allow your true essence to rise from within and flow freely. With renewed thoughts, you realign yourself with who you truly are, a marvelous being, connected to God, the orchestrating Power that sustains the universe.

From this level of consciousness, you feel joy in co-creating the desires of your heart with God, the Highest Power, the Alpha and Omega. You acknowledge the depth of his love for you.

As you journey, you are attuned to his infinite wisdom that inspires and guides you. You recognize that he aligns people and events to ease your journey. You are hopeful for tomorrow and excited for the abundant possibilities that each day brings. Lasting joy lives in your heart each day.

Power Thought

In God's hand, I find comfort. My heart is filled with glee as he guides each and every step of my life.

Jocelyne F. Lafrenière

Day 55

Learn from yesterday's mistakes for more success tomorrow.

Whenever your heart dances to the "Life is Good" song, you feel good about who you are and what you want. You are passionate and excited about life. You give yourself permission to grow, thus allowing you to make mistakes in the process.

If you commit a misstep or did not choose the right path, you are not overly critical of yourself. Learn what needs to be learned, and move on. See setbacks for what they are: opportunities to learn and identify new paths to travel by, moments to make better choices, and occasions to be creative, confident, and perseverant.

With great determination, you design a new action plan. You move towards your vision with feel-good thoughts and positive beliefs. With God by your side, you take your next steps with confidence. Soon you will reach new heights of success.

Power Thought

My heart sings a song of happiness. Life is good,
and each day is a new beginning.

 *Day 56*

Intuition is your trusted friend.

You are born to be a visionary, an influencer, and a powerful creator, not an observer of the universe with no control over your life. You are fully equipped to become who you are meant to be. You are gifted with discernment, inner wisdom, and knowingness.

If a desire is lingering in your heart, it means it is yours to fulfill. Know without any doubt that infinite wisdom is behind your desire. Desires from the heart are blessings coming towards you and those around you.

Activate your *True Inspiration* app. Relax your mind and tune in to your intuition. Let it be your trusted friend. Pay attention to the omens scattered along your path that provide divine guidance. Most importantly, follow your heart, and you will find happy surprises coming your way. Soon, your life will turn around, with aliveness and inner joy flowing in your heart for simply allowing yourself to be.

Power Thought

I follow my heart, and I know that happy surprises are coming my way.

 *Day 57*

With the eyes of the heart, you see the beauty in others.

God made each one of us unique and special as a celebration of the diversity that he is. In his eyes, we are all beings of great value, a divine expression of his life.

Uniquely gifted with skills and talents, we are meant to be a delight to those around us. When we fulfill our life mission and purpose, we release our sweet aroma into the universe. We bring enthusiasm, passion, and energy, and make this world a better place.

With the eyes of the heart, you can see this uniqueness in others and celebrate diversity. You appreciate and value their distinctive contributions and gifts. You see diversity of personalities, ideas, genders, cultures, races, and ethnicities as enrichment. You understand that diversity is the basis for expansion. You are reminded that we are all one.

Power Thought

As a being of love, I embrace diversity. I strive for respect, compassion, and the well-being of all.

Day 58

Unlock your passion to create your dream of a better tomorrow.

With *High Drive* turned on, you claim your full power, leading you to actively pursue the desires of your heart. You are passionate about using your gifts and skills to better your life and the lives of those around you.

You are motivated to craft a roadmap to get you to your destination in less time. You figure out ingenious initiatives to achieve your desires. With your contingency plan in hand, you are not intimidated by roadblocks.

With *High Drive*, you release the hand brake and move into action with commitment, self-control, and perseverance to live your best life. You are excited to be alive, speeding ahead with high productivity and effectiveness. You increase power when going up a hill, and you celebrate each milestone toward your destination. Buckled up, you enjoy the ride. With a positive outlook on life, race ahead and maintain your vision.

Power Thought

I choose to create the desires of my heart. I am ready for an amazing ride on the road to success.

Jocelyne F. Lafrenière

 *Day 59*

Life is a thrilling adventure. Enjoy the journey, one step at a time.

Your journey is an exciting adventure, with challenges and new beginnings for your greatest transformation. Embrace setbacks with a spirit of gratitude, and trust that all will be well.

You are armed with courage, strength, and resilience, fully equipped to bounce back quickly from adversity. By standing strong in the face of life's disappointments, your mind and soul delve in positivity, and you keep depression and discouragement at bay. Your heart sings a song of joyful expectations.

If you failed the first time, be willing to dream again and dream big. Be willing to try again. The road to your dream may be long and paved with rocks, but don't give up. Keep walking and you will reach your dream. God will bring to fruition the seeds of greatness that he has planted in you.

Power Thought

I am not afraid of setbacks. Challenges enable me to rise higher. I trust the grander plan of life.

 *Day* 60

Life's annoyances have no grip on you. Unbounded joy lives in your heart.

The storms of life—the loss of a loved one, the loss of a job, a scarce financial situation, shattered desires, or a divorce—can be debilitating and open the door for depression to swoop in.

Remember that you are *Marvelous You*, connected to the Life Power that created the universe. You are not alone as the winds blow on your life. He is always with you, and he sustains you with his unwavering love. He will never abandon you. He will forge a way forward for you and calm the sea in due time.

Stand strong through the storm as you await his perfect timing. Let him fill your heart with hope and peace. God has brought you this far; he will not forsake you. Smile. A rainbow will soon color your life.

Power Thought

I let my soul take refuge in God as I weather the storms of life. Serenity flows in my heart as springs of living water. I wait in peace for God's rainbow to light up my life.

 *Day 61*

Enjoy today; don't be anxious about tomorrow, as it is not here yet.

There are moments in life when your mind and heart are plagued with anxiety. You can't think or reason properly. You worry about everything, founded or unfounded. You expect disaster, and you only see darkness. You cry, and you are desperate. You are totally debilitated, with extreme nervousness and uneasiness day after day. You no longer function at work or at home, and you have serious difficulties interacting with others.

When anxiety engulfs your heart, return to God. By harnessing the Highest Power of the universe in faith, open your heart and cast your concerns on him. He communicates with you in different ways: through nature, people, experiences, intuition, inspiration, music, prayer, and inspiring writings and teachings. Reach out to him. His hand is waiting for yours.

With your mind and heart well anchored in God, your thoughts and emotions will be renewed. He will give you all you need to tackle tomorrow, and he will sustain you by his grace.

Power Thought

I stay in harmony with God, with peace and hope in my heart. I trust that tomorrow, and the next day, and the next will work out for my own good.

Day 62

Surround yourself with positive and uplifting people.

If you want to move forward, say goodbye to negative people who do not share or respect your core values, who use you for their own benefit, bring your energy down, and leave you feeling stressed or suffocated. Say hello to those who believe in your greatness and uplift you.

Surround yourself with people who are successful, objective, non-judgmental, and have your interests at heart. Like-minded, positive people recognize your value. They believe in you and support you as you take steps to achieve your dreams.

Their positive energy is contagious, and their enthusiasm lifts you up. They rejoice with you while you celebrate successes. Their kind words of encouragement and wisdom are all you need to keep you motivated as you journey through your life.

Power Thought

I surround myself with people who are positive, uplifting, and believe in me. I let go of people who bring my energy down and use me.

 *Day 63*

By planting seeds of love, you bring a smile to people's hearts.

Love is the best symphony; you can play along with people from all ethnicities, cultures, and religions. You are a living expression of God. Through you, he bestows kindness to others.

Richly blessed with love, you are a nurturer who never ceases to care for others. You emanate generosity, patience, forgiveness, and compassion. You love unconditionally through kind words and actions that inspire understanding, trust, support, and openness. You make others feel safe, and you respect their personal journey towards healing and wholeness. By spreading your wings of love you bring more peace, hope, and light into the world.

Activate your *Love Power* app, and be the love that you are meant to be. A smile, a hug, a compliment, and even an attentive ear are all perfect ways to make other people feel loved. By nourishing relationships with kind words, caring actions, truthfulness, forgiveness, and compassion, you will make this world a better place.

Power Thought

I am love in action, and I radiate kindness, patience, forgiveness, and compassion. Today, I will plant seeds of love around me.

 *Day 64*

Friendship is a precious treasure.

There is joy in developing new friendships and mutual sharing. A big smile with a thank you or hello is all you need to create a connection. Reaching out to someone else sets the stage for expansion to take place in both your and the other person's life.

True friends see the good in you and appreciate your gifts and talents. They enrich your life with a sense of worth, belonging, and confidence, which you reciprocate. They are your best cheerleaders, offering support and encouragement in times of need. They listen without judgment and speak words of wisdom.

Real friendships live in your heart and never leave you. They don't dwindle due to time or distance. Moments together are embraced with memories, sharing, and laughter.

Cherish your friendships and nourish them with care, kindness, and respect. Let yourself be a breeze of kindness and positive energy in your friends' lives.

Power Thought

*Life has given me true friends. I am richly blessed
with these priceless gifts and I cherish them.*

 *Day 65*

Each day is a new beginning.

Are you living day by day without any passion or excitement? Do you feel stuck, unable to move forward? If you are ready to give your life another chance and experience greater fulfillment, turn on your *True Inspiration* app today and fire up your mind with inspiration to create an amazing life. It's time to go back to the drawing board and set a new vision and inspiring goals.

Don't be afraid to change your life. With *True Inspiration* turned on, find the why and how behind what you want to do. Craft an action plan and get in gear to find greater satisfaction and fulfillment in your life. You are meant to live to the utmost of your greatness. You have the power to direct your intentions and actions toward your dreams. You deserve happiness and success.

Have faith in tomorrow. Get excited for another day of possibilities, opportunities, and experiences. Trust in the grander plan of life. Life is a thrilling adventure with new beginnings for your greatest transformation.

Power Thought

*I take charge of my life. I choose to create the life I
want. I take action to change my tomorrows.*

 *Day 66*

You are endowed with unique beauty.

You are gifted with your own abilities and competencies. Do not try to be someone you are not meant to be. It will drain your energies and leave you unproductive, stressed, and unhealthy. Learn to love yourself with your personal beauty.

You are a marvelous being, born to achieve your aspirations with your body, soul, and spirit. Success is all about you discovering your gifts and talents, learning and growing, being creative, taking action, and adding more beauty into the universe.

You are creativity when you are inspired with ideas. You are passion when you get excited about your new projects. You are pure joy when you rejoice for no reason. You are courage when you bounce back from adversity. You are wisdom when you take action for the betterment of all. Be gracious and honor your own uniqueness. Let it shine for all to see.

Power Thought

I embrace all that I am, with my unique gifts and abilities. Driven by my life purpose, I move toward my desires with passion.

 *Day 67*

By setting an intention that moves you, you activate the manifestation process.

You hold the power to allow your life to flourish and live your deepest aspirations. All come into play in the manifestation process: inspired thoughts, a winning strategy, focused actions, unwavering faith in God, and positive emotions.

Your thoughts are the sparks that ignite the manifestation process. With a clear intention well aligned with your belief, set a strategy and step into action. Focused and determined, stand strong in the face of adversity. With daily affirmations and creative visualization, move forward with confidence in the direction of your desires. Faith moves you to an even higher vibration of energy, where you find greater confidence.

Embraced by good feelings, you are in a state of positive expectancy. You are grateful for what is to come, trusting that all will be well.

Power Thought

With confidence, I give life to my aspirations by moving into action. Faith and feel-good thoughts sustain me through the journey.

 *Day 68*

Fear is a lie of your mind.

You are not fear; you are the *Marvelous You*, fearless and peaceful. Crush the fear of failure and not being good enough. Stop listening to those lies. Get out there and with a positive attitude and motivation, show the world what you are capable of doing.

Let living to your full potential be part of your legacy. If you miss the mark and get hurt, then learn from the experience and try again. Most successful people and great leaders have stories of trials and tribulations, and they all share the same determination, courage, and resilience to pursue their desires.

You are born to be a success. Be willing to take a risk and embrace the unknown. Be remembered as a conqueror who was willing to learn and overcame fears and mistakes. Embrace challenges. Don't just give up in the face of glitches. Be patient with yourself and others. Obstacles are nothing more than opportunities for growth.

Power Thought

I stay on course day after day. I move forward with assertive actions to turn my dreams into reality.

Jocelyne F. Lafrenière

 *Day 69*

You either master your thoughts or they master you.

Each day is full of external events that impact your life, and your response to these events influences your emotional temperature. It can go up or down as you respond favorably or not to life events and annoyances. Not knowing how to master your emotions is like being at sea without a life jacket. You will soon drown, swept away by the high waves.

You hold the power to radiate more love, joy, enthusiasm, and bliss in your life. With your *Dynamo* app activated, you can take control over toxic emotions and say goodbye to anxiety, anger, rage, bitterness, depression, and despair. As you go about your day, turn on your happy thoughts. Feel-good thoughts move you from low- to high-vibration feelings.

If one feel-good thought is not enough, then choose another one until you are at peace and well-anchored in your well-being zone. Practice makes perfect, so don't be discouraged if you have occasional negative thoughts and you feel sad, disappointed, fearful, or upset for a moment. Simply replace your thoughts with better ones, and realign yourself for a more harmonious life.

Power Thought

*I choose to only have happy thoughts. In turn,
I radiate joy and bliss in my life.*

 *Day 70*

You can't change the past, but you can change tomorrow.

Life's disappointments can be like tsunamis that extinguish your inner spark. From spouse betrayal to wrongful dismissal to shattered desires, life's setbacks can be brutal to withstand, especially when they involve other people who have hurt you.

If holding a grudge is your *spark extinguisher*, invite forgiveness into your heart. Forgiveness means moving forward despite your hurts. Letting go of the past heals your wounds and gives you wings to fly.

If your *spark extinguisher* is a lost dream or a roadblock, do not lose sight of who you are, a marvelous being. Roadblocks are challenges to overcome, not to paralyze you. Pull out your contingency plan and get into action. Feed your disappointments with small actions and faith. You will soon fire yourself back up.

Power Thought

I have great expectations for what is to come. I stand strong in my commitment to live my best life.

Jocelyne F. Lafrenière

 *Day 71*

By embracing positivity, you live life with more ease.

Feeling down, disappointed, or discouraged? It's time to enlighten your life—thoughts, behavior, words, faith, and values—with positivity. By maintaining a positive outlook, you nourish your mind with feel-good thoughts that raise your vibrations and move you to your well-being zone.

With a positive attitude, you move in life with more confidence, courage, and passion. You are grateful for today and for what is yet to come. You speak words of possibilities and become your own best friend. You tame your inner critic and congratulate yourself for your successes, small and grand.

Well-grounded in God, your heart is safe in true joy. In oneness with him, your soul is enlightened. You experience acceptance, wholeness, and harmony. In this communion, praise is on your lips each day. You put little feet under your values and walk the talk. You bring to the world more goodness and light. You extend acts of kindness around you.

Power Thought

I fly to new heights of well-being by embracing a positive attitude.

 *Day 72*

Do not be overpowered by challenges and suffering. Be empowered by them.

Challenges and suffering are opportunities for growth, not defeat and sadness. Whether you lost your job, are going through a divorce, or encounter a scarce financial situation, challenges allow you to become stronger, fearless, courageous, and more in control of your thoughts.

Suffering opens the door to more compassion and a deeper love for those who are going through similar experiences, whether it's the loss of a loved one, sickness, a shattered desire, or other painful experiences.

You have the ability to overcome what comes your way. With faith, you can keep moving on. God is with you, and he understands your pains and sorrows. He will hold your hand as you take your next steps. Know that there is a light at the end of the tunnel and keep walking, no matter what. Today does not define your tomorrow.

Power Thought

Challenges and suffering make me a better person.
I welcome them rather than fight them.

 *Day 73*

Me time each day keeps anxiety away.

Prolonged stress or stressful events can lead to depression, sleep disorders, and anxiety. Taking *Me* time each day to care for yourself, de-stress, and feel more energized helps you stay in your well-being zone for a more vibrant life.

Activate your *Fun and Play* app to bring more leisure time into your life. Plan for a few *Me* time activities in your day. If time is scarce, then choose to do at least one activity that is just for you. Soon you will feel more alive and your life will be brighter. Do daily stretches, light calisthenics, breathing exercises, or other relaxation and nurturing techniques. Read inspiring books and positive affirmations, engage in visualization and praising prayer.

Write in your gratitude journal, listen to inspiring music, step outside for a brisk walk to witness nature around you, take a warm bath, or get a soothing massage. Even if you cannot sleep, take naps or just relax in bed. Give your body time to rest and recuperate. Calm your racing mind in any possible ways that work for you for your greater well-being.

Power Thought

*I take Me time each day to bring peace to my mind
and soul, and to transform my day into a marvelous
experience with more energy and harmony.*

Day 74

Mindfulness is a gift to yourself.

Stop for a moment. Take a few deep breaths and observe what is happening around you. What sounds do you hear? What do you see? What do you smell? How do you feel? What do you think? By bringing your attention to your thoughts, emotions, body, and senses in this present moment, you have just practiced mindfulness.

Mindfulness is a calm awareness of life in all its beauty, with its past and present moments. It can be practiced as you take a walk during your lunch hour, while on the bus to work, or during your work break.

By focusing on the present moment, you feel the energy of life within you and around you. You are reminded that you are part of this vast universe, connected to all other human beings, animals, and nature. The eyes of your heart open and you see that all is in you to create an amazing life: abundance, creativity, glee, peace, and love.

Don't wait any longer to let mindfulness be part of your day Not only will it increase your physical, emotional, and spiritual well-being, but it will revive a sense of awe at life.

Power Thought

I let mindfulness be part of each of my days for greater well-being.

Jocelyne F. Lafrenière

 *Day 75*

Change comes when you create it.

Taking ownership of your life involves being responsible for what you create with your thoughts, emotions, and actions. It means having faith in your ability to co-create a better future with the Highest Power of the universe. If you want change in your life and don't see much happening, search inside of you where the answers lie. It is in the silence and the quietness of your heart that you will find inspiration and guidance.

For some people, avoiding the same negative outcomes may entail changing the way they do things. For others, it may mean that they need to let go of past events and insecurity that influence their today.

Change comes when you take ownership of it. Oftentimes, people believe that their fate is caused by someone other than themselves. They blame their father or mother, they blame their spouse or ex-spouse, or they blame their employer or their peers. Any reason is used to shun facing reality, taking responsibility for their actions, and changing what needs to be changed. In true honesty, listen to your heart and take charge of your life to be all that you can be.

Power Thought

*I welcome change in my life. I dare to dream bigger
dreams for the full flourishing of my life.*

Day 76

Each day is a moment to grow and discover your great beauty.

Each one of us is gifted. You are called to transform yourself and create a fulfilling life for you and those around you. Don't hide your gifts. Develop new skills, open your mind to new ideas, find the creativity within you, try new things, and let your voice be heard. These are all great ways to let your light shine.

If your heart is filled with desires and hopes, don't ignore them. Desires are often messages of the direction you should be taking for your life, and they always come with the power to realize them.

If you want more in your life, then make choices that will attract abundance. You want more love? Love more. You want more friends? Be more of a friend. You want more money? Give more. You want more kindness? Care more. You want more blessings? Be more grateful. By being more of what you want, you become a magnet who attracts more of what you yearn for. As you attract more, give more. In doing so, you are creating a powerful circle of abundance.

Power Thought

I am the success I want to be. I am full of creativity, autonomy, passion, and love.

Jocelyne F. Lafrenière

 *Day 77*

By letting go of what does not serve you, you enrich your life.

You want true love in your life? More friends? More money? More health? Today is the day to take action and open your arms to receive what is best for you. By letting go of what does not serve you, you make room for what will enrich and uplift your life.

Stepping away from unrequited love opens the door to a new love and true companionships. As you walk away from loneliness, you attract more friends. By recognizing that money is a blessing, you create a prosperity mind-set. By saying goodbye to unhealthy habits, you invite more wellness and vitality into your life.

There is magic in the letting go process. Not only do you attract more, but you are in a position to give more. You have the power to create a powerful circle of abundance in your life and the lives of others.

Power Thought

I activate the power of letting go of what does not serve me. I make room physically, emotionally, and spiritually for more to come into my life.

 *Day 78*

Let your light shine.

As you grow in awareness of your *Marvelous Nature*, you will be inspired to live to the fullest with your body, soul, and spirit. In doing so, you will invite abundance into your life at all levels: physically, emotionally, intellectually, financially, and spiritually.

You are imbued with talents, skills, and abilities to bring more beauty into the world. By activating your *True Inspiration* app, inspiration will flow abundantly to help you become all that you can be. You will master the ability to tune in to your intuition to actualize your life purpose.

With feel-good thoughts and inspired actions, you will create a purpose-driven life. As you unlock your full potential, you will light up the world with all that you are. All this is for you and those around you to experience greater fulfillment, joyousness, and well-being.

As you discover Spirit, you see the invisible. In faith, you expect great things to happen and stay in a state of constant gratitude. You praise the Infinite Power of the universe who co-creates with you.

Power Thought

In oneness with God, I continue to grow in perfection and delight in him.

Jocelyne F. Lafrenière

 *Day 79*

Open the gates of your heart and let love flow in abundance.

Everyone is subject to pain, sadness, and bruises inflicted by someone else. Oftentimes, other people's own bruises make them say and do things out of fear rather than out of love. As a result, they bruise those around them and create more sadness and pain. They act from their own level of consciousness, making decisions and speaking words that reflect their current level of awareness.

Forgiveness is an act towards emotional freedom. You make that choice because you yearn for wholeness and well-being. You forgive those who have wronged or abused you to set *yourself* free. You wish to set others free to make mistakes, experience life, and unfold their *Marvelous Self* in their own time.

Gently open your heart to God. His divine power of love and forgiveness will flow within you to clear negative emotions. Anger towards those who have hurt you will be released for more harmony in your body, soul, and spirit.

Power Thought

I choose to forgive those who wronged me so my
soul can be a garden of well-being.

Day 80

Get your fire back.

There are moments in life when disappointments can become so overwhelming that you wonder if life is worth living. You feel lost and your soul is engulfed by darkness.

Whatever reason is behind your loss of enthusiasm and excitement for life, know that you can bounce back. Remind yourself that you are the *Marvelous You*, born to be a visionary and a powerful creator, not just an observer of life. Take time to reflect on what you want your life to be and who you want to be.

Try to understand how you went from flying high to flying low. With greater clarity on your *spark extinguishers*, you will reenergize yourself. You are pure creativity, fully equipped to live your best life. Don't let self-oppression and self-doubt stop you from creating your best life. As you get your fire back, you will warm up the world with your sparks of energy, excitement, and love.

Power Thought

I commit to myself and choose to live my best life, no matter what.

Jocelyne F. Lafrenière

 *Day 81*

You are the movie writer, director, and producer of your destiny.

If you have a desire in your heart, it means you have the resources to create it. Inspiration is the spark that ignites the transformation process and creates a chain reaction that produces positive results. By focusing on what you want, your thoughts produce high vibrations in the energy space, with feelings of excitement, passion, and hope in your body that move you into action.

If you don't like your life as it is now, challenge your thoughts and beliefs. By choosing better-feeling thoughts and beliefs, you say goodbye to hopelessness, boredom, discouragement, frustration, resentment, failure, and fear.

You are the *Marvelous You*, and you are armed to live your best life. By keeping your thoughts in alignment with your desires, you gain better control over your life. You are no longer a victim controlled by life, circumstances, or actions of others. You are a conqueror living victoriously in full freedom and control over your thoughts and actions.

Power Thought

I keep my mind captive in feel-good thoughts and create the life I want.

 *Day 82*

As you let Spirit lead your life, you awaken to divine bliss.

You are connected to the stupendous Power that sustains all there is in the universe. Whether you acknowledge it or not, this Life Force is always guiding you while you journey through your life. You are endowed with free will, and God has lovingly intended for you to reach out to him for companionship.

By activating your *Higher Power* app, you ignite a spiritual, dynamic, and interactive relationship with God. You consciously acknowledge him as the Ultimate Source, the All-That-Is, and the Alpha and Omega. You recognize his supremacy over both the physical and spiritual worlds.

In oneness with him, your soul is divinely enlightened. You gain a better understanding of the grander plan of life. You truly capture that your true purpose in life is to actualize your *Marvelous Self* for more glee and well-being in your life and the world around you.

Power Thought

As I embrace Spirit, I realize oneness with him. As I feed from Spirit, I experience wholeness.

 *Day 83*

Gratitude is that place of the heart that celebrates life.

It is hard to be grateful when one storm after another hits you with disappointments, losses, break-ups, or scarcity. If a storm hits outside, don't let it hit you inside. Let gratitude be your soul armor against despair.

There is tremendous power in thankfulness. It wakes up positivity, happiness, hope, and faith. With a grateful heart, you are thankful for realizing your true purpose and becoming the best that you can be. You appreciate all the small joys that each day brings, as well as the love that you receive and give. You are thankful for your unique gifts and talents, and how you have used them for your own fulfillment and the betterment of others.

By being grateful for all aspects of your life, you make room for more inner joy and peace. Pains and sorrows are no longer your enemies; they are teachers of compassion for others. Don't forget, you are rich in talents, friends, love, and all good things. True abundance is in you and around you.

Power Thought

I am grateful for all that I learn as I walk through the storms of life.
I trust that God will pave a way forward for my life to be fruitful.

 *Day 84*

Sow good seeds for future generations to reap the benefits.

Caring for tomorrow is an expression of love towards the universe, your children, your community, your country, and generations to come. It is conscious awareness that what you do today lives on, and that your thoughts and actions make a difference. It's the understanding that planet Earth is not yours, and you are simply a visitor for a brief time.

Caring for those to come means setting aside your personal needs for the greater good. It's all about those daily choices that will make a difference in future people's lives, whether it's a *green* action or supporting diversity and equality.

By caring today, you will change tomorrow. You will enable future generations to have the resources to live their best lives with lasting peace, respect, and equal rights and opportunities. You will teach them to cherish the utmost respect for planet Earth and humankind, which in turn will create a better future for those who will come after.

Power Thought

I am a drop in the ocean of life that makes
a difference for those to come.

Jocelyne F. Lafrenière

 *Day 85*

With little feet under your desires, you will reach your destination.

You are here to affirm all that you are, and your contribution to this world is totally unique. Being from God and in God, your life is meant to be a great adventure with meaning and value for yourself, those around you, and those that will come after you.

You are called to live life to the fullest and pursue your aspirations. Light up your inner fire today. Listen to the still, small voice of your heart where your aspirations are waiting to come alive.

Desires with no little feet will lead you nowhere. Simply drifting along will not bring excitement, passion, and success into your life. Feed your mind with feel-good thoughts and get into action today. By achieving your goals one step at a time with a positive attitude, you will progress toward your destination with less effort. When you live your truth, you make your greatest contribution to this world: the gift of all that you are.

Power Thought

I choose to be all that I can be. I am abundance. I am creativity. I am joy. I am courage.

 *Day 86*

Free will is a powerful tool to be used wisely to avoid spinning out of control.

You were born with free will as your birthright. You bear full responsibility for what you create with your thoughts, beliefs, emotions, and actions. When you choose love, forgiveness, confidence, and joy, you bring to light your *Marvelous Essence*. By choosing disrespect, hate, anger, despair, and worry, you are drifting away from the *Marvelous You* and becoming the *powerless you.*

Gifted with free will, you can either create goodness and beauty or create oppression, violence, war, chaos, and suffering. You play a dominant role in what you create. Thus, you are called to choose wisely and responsibly, with love as your ultimate guidance.

Free will with love is powerful, but free will without love is disastrous. Not choosing love has dire consequences for you and those around you. Turn on your *Love Power* app today to bring more light to this world.

Power Thought

I choose wisely and create love around me, for the betterment of all.

 *Day 87*

By keeping your conscious mind busy with feel-good thoughts, you are giving wings to your life.

You are endowed with freedom to choose your beliefs and values. If you are plagued with beliefs and values that no longer resonate with you, then take charge and choose to counteract their effects. While past beliefs can't be removed, you can create new ones to actualize the exciting life you deserve.

Start by reflecting on new beliefs that would move you in the direction of your desires. Then plant these new beliefs in your mind with positive affirmations and visualization.

By reading positive affirmations about your *Marvelous Nature* each day, renewed thoughts will be transferred to your subconscious mind and stored as your new beliefs. The process is even more powerful when your affirmations trigger positive emotions, such as glee, confidence, and excitement.

Empower the benefits of reading your positive affirmations with daily visualization. Close your eyes and visualize each attribute of your *Marvelous Nature*. With more awareness of who you truly are, you will experience wholeness and well-being.

Power Thought

My life is abundant in every way. Each moment is a moment to rejoice.

 *Day 88*

Be comfortable being uncomfortable.

Don't be intimidated by change. Being uncomfortable simply means you are on your way to being all that you can be by developing new skills, trying new activities, and meeting new people. To easily navigate in the uncomfortable zone, first open your mind to who you truly are, the *Marvelous You*, engaged and enthusiastic to explore all possibilities that lie within you. Acknowledge your potential to do amazing things and be ready to replace limiting beliefs with new ones.

Take mini-steps out of your comfort zone to become more comfortable doing the uncomfortable. See each action, challenge, and experience as an occasion to learn, grow, and be creative. Don't forget to keep your emotions under control to ease discomfort from fears that may capture your heart and mind.

Connected to the organizing Power that sustains the universe, nourish a mind-set that has faith in your abilities and in God to take you to a place of growth and fulfillment. By mastering your thoughts, you will move to the high zone of the emotion spectrum where you experience hope and enthusiasm as you embrace change.

Power Thought

I happily welcome change and live life to the fullest. Faith opens my eyes to a world of new possibilities for my life.

Jocelyne F. Lafrenière

 *Day 89*

Dance to the music of your heart.

You were born to be the creator of your life, not to dance to someone else's tune. You were not born to relinquish control of your life. You were given the gift of volition to choose who you want to be and what you want to achieve in life.

You are gifted with your own life purpose and mission. Your life is yours to create. Don't let anyone tell you otherwise. In silencing who you are, you are depriving the world of your great beauty. It takes lots of courage to stand up for yourself and take your life back.

Resolve to fight for your birthright and enjoy your free will. Strange as it seems, you will be surprised by how much respect people will have for you as you stand for your desires and convictions. Set an example as to what life is meant to be. Life is short; live *your* dreams, not someone else's.

Power Thought

I honor who I am and my aspirations. I deserve to create my best life, and I follow my heart.

 *Day 90*

Rejoice for an exciting journey on the path to success

Each of your experiences, good and bad, is an opportunity for growth. Challenges are opportunities for your creativity to emerge. In addition, they may hold a message that there is a faster or better path ahead.

A positive attitude will move you faster to your destination. Rejoicing means knowing that God is with you through hardship. It means giving thanks for what is to come and being being patient, disciplined, and perseverant.

Rejoicing keeps doubts and fears away. Your mind is filled with creative thoughts and new ideas to handle challenges. Your heart overflows with hope, enthusiasm, and optimism, knowing that hard times will pass. You believe that the impossible is indeed possible. Each step in the direction of your dreams, whether small or grand, is a blessing. It makes the journey fun and joyful.

Power Thought

I trust that all is good, knowing that in each challenge there is a lesson to be learned. God will bring to completion what he has started.

Jocelyne F. Lafrenière

 *Day 91*

Reaching out is a gift of love to you and those around you.

As the *Marvelous You*, the world is your home and mankind your brethren. You enjoy reaching out to others to create moments of happiness. You serve using your abilities for the betterment of others. You share who you are and what you have.

With your caring and listening skills, you are attuned to other people's needs. You foster hope and courage in those who are facing difficult times. As you give and receive love, you experience a sense of belonging. You discover the great beauty in others. Simply put, reaching out is the experience of openness and of deep connections that enrich your life in so many ways. It is a source of fulfillment and a blessing for you and others.

Be a light unto someone else's path and let the other person's sunshine brighten your life. Embrace these moments of togetherness for both of your glows to outshine darkness.

Power Thought

I make beautiful music in the lives of those around me. I create a powerful circle of abundance.

 *Day 92*

Let wisdom be your signature.

Wisdom comes when you pause and listen to your inner voice, letting the Highest Power of the universe flow within your heart and guide you while you journey through your life. In nourishing your connection to God you are attuned to his voice, not strictly acting on your own knowledge and judgment.

As you create your legacy of wisdom, reflect on the beauties and wonders of life. Reflect on how you have grown and what you have learned over the years. Reflect on where you are and the direction you want to take.

Wisdom comes when you reckon you know so little and there is always more to learn. Strive for excellence, not perfection. Give yourself and others some room to explore and make mistakes. Celebrate all that you are and have accomplished. While you journey through your life, laugh, cry, celebrate, and learn.

Power Thought

Wisdom emanates from each of my experiences, failures, and successes.

Jocelyne F. Lafrenière

 *Day 93*

Like a caterpillar, all is in you to become a beautiful butterfly, free to rise to new heights.

Expressing your *Marvelous Self* is a transforming process that gradually takes place as you experience life. At a very early age, you discovered your creativity. You were curious and explored the world around you.

In your teenage years your instincts, passions, and aspirations became stronger. You were hopeful and confident for the future. Now you are fearless, not shying away from new experiences. Love is smiling at you, and you smile back. Through life experiences, you discover your unique gifts and talents. You joyfully create your own life experiences with inspiration and wisdom. You discover the beauties of life, and your heart is filled with gratefulness.

By cultivating spiritual awareness, you attain conscious oneness with God. From that place flows true love that you freely share with humanity. Connected to the Highest Power of the universe, you expand your mind and you are directed in life with divine inspiration and intuition. Through this transformational process, you discover your true self in its full beauty.

Power Thought

I fly high like an arrow in the sky. With my wings wide open, I discover my true beauty.

 *Day 94*

When you close your eyes to this world, let love be your greatest legacy.

You are a beautiful human being, connected to the Life Force that sustains the universe. You are here on planet Earth to allow your true essence, the *Marvelous You*, to emerge in all its beauty. You are wonderfully gifted with the power to love. When you activate your *Love Power* app, you transform not only your life but the lives of others.

You appreciate and value those around you, with their unique contributions and gifts. With an open heart, you create loving, harmonious, and fulfilling relationships. With your thoughts and actions captive in love, you make better choices that reflect compassion and forgiveness, which in turn enlighten the world.

You experience much joy and fulfillment in receiving and giving love to your family, friends, and communities. You emanate kindness, acceptance, patience, understanding, and compassion. You travel light by forgiving those who have abused or wronged you, understanding that everyone is on a path of learning and growing. *All* of you is love: your speech, actions, mind, and heart.

Power Thought

I let the power of love transform my life. My speech is love.
My actions are love. Kindness is my signature.

Jocelyne F. Lafrenière

 *Day 95*

We create war by ignoring the sacredness of life and the right to freedom.

Wars, environmental issues, and economic crises are created out of fear, not out of love. They are born from a place of limited understanding of life and abundance. It is only in the actualization of our *Marvelous Nature* that we will resolve the chaos we have created.

We create war by ignoring the sacredness of life and the right to freedom. We create famine by protecting ourselves first and letting others take care of themselves. We wrongly believe that wealth is limited, and spreading it around would leave us in a precarious position. We create air and land pollution, global warming, and resource depletion by focusing on today's gain with no respect for tomorrow.

Choose wisely and create your life in a spirit of love for the betterment of your family, community, country, and those to come after you. All it takes is a conscious shift towards love, reverence for life, unity, peace, freedom, international cooperation, and Earth preservation.

Power Thought

I choose wisely and radiate love at home, at work, and in my community, developing friendships, sharing my gifts, and serving others.

Day 96

Be an angel in someone else's life.

If you want your heart to sing again, activate your *Love Power* app today. Love will fill your life with a new song. With *Love Power*, you appreciate and value those around you, with their unique contributions and gifts. You discover the power of goodness and you experience much joy and fulfillment in receiving and giving love to your family, friends, partners, and the world.

There are no riches as deep as love. Those we remember and continue to celebrate are those who have touched our hearts with their love. As you journey through your life, let your love shine. Let the power of kindness, forgiveness, compassion, and love for yourself and others flow abundantly. Not only will you happily transform *your* world, but you transform *the* world.

By creating a legacy of love, you will be cherished for your contribution to making this world a better place, and your life will be a source of inspiration to others.

Power Thought

Like a waterfall, I let cascades of love flow over people around me.

Jocelyne F. Lafrenière

 *Day 97*

Create a legacy of self-love and acceptance.

You are the *Marvelous You*, an extension of Infinite Love. As a being of love, you deserve to cultivate self-love and let it be a part of your legacy. Loving yourself is honoring all that you are with your body, soul, and spirit. In doing so, you are telling the world that you are a beautiful and worthy human being.

Self-love is unconditional acceptance of all that you are, with your strengths, weaknesses, and physical traits you love, and those you try to hide. It is honoring your aspirations and trusting in your own judgment and intuition. It is embracing each of your life's experiences, the good and not so good, knowing that you are a work in progress.

Self-love is not letting yourself be drowned by negative comments and people. It is the force that makes you say no to verbal and physical abuse. It is taking care of yourself day in and day out and bringing more fitness, vigor, and well-being into your life.

Power Thought

I am a beautiful human being, worthy of love,
and especially worthy of my love.

Day 98

Everything is possible to those who believe in the impossible.

Life is a treasure chest filled with riches that are your aspirations, experiences, successes, loved ones, and all those simple little joys of life that you create each and every day.

As you experience life, bury all your positive experiences in your treasure chest. Each day, open it and celebrate the growth you've made; your successes, special moments with family and friends, the knowledge you've gained, the gifts you have, the better control you have over your finances, and the love you share and receive.

When you look into your treasure chest, you reinforce your beliefs in success, reminding yourself of your past wins, the possibilities that are in you, and the beauties of life. Self-confidence is key to personal success. With confidence comes positive emotions that move you forward. Believing in yourself is a powerful choice that allows you to accomplish great things and be a success. Celebrating small and big wins is a great way to build self-confidence.

Power Thought

Positive memories remind me that I am a wonderful being with great potential. I am creative, confident, and fearless.

Jocelyne F. Lafrenière

 *Day 99*

As you expand your awareness, you enrich your present moment.

Life is all about expansion. As you expand your horizons, you grow. As you live new experiences, your subconscious mind expands. As you expand your awareness, you soar to new heights of consciousness.

You are wired for more goodness and less hardship. Look at how you relate to money. Do you want less money? Of course not; you want more. How about health and free time? Do you want less? The answer is no and no; you want more. You are joy and goodness in expansion.

You are a powerful creator equipped to create the desires of your heart. You are born to expand your capacities, blossom, and realize your *Marvelous Nature*. Do more of what you love. Turn the power on and expand your life for more glee, love, success, and well-being. Love yourself and be grateful for your own gifts.

Power Thought

I am born to expand my capacities, blossom, and realize my Marvelous Nature.

Day 100

Not only will faith change your world, but it will change the world.

Faith is a celebration of life, of who you are, a powerful creator connected to other human beings and God. Faith is a gift that you receive upon birth; it's an amazing force that lives in you. Through expanded consciousness let faith in yourself, in others, in tomorrow, and in the impossible, evolve and grow.

Faith in yourself is an expression of self-love. It means you have captured the beauty of all that you are with your unique talents, capabilities, and potential. Faith in others recognizes the same beauty in others who, just like you, experience life with its good and not-so-good moments.

Faith in tomorrow keeps you walking, knowing there is light at the end of the tunnel. It keeps your heart hopeful for a better tomorrow as you go through life's dark moments. It makes you see each experience as an opportunity for personal growth and new awareness. Faith in God keeps your lips praising his greatness. It whispers in your ear that you belong to a higher purpose, even though your human consciousness cannot grasp it all at this time.

Power Thought

I let my faith be a celebration of life. Kindness, hope,
inner joy, and harmony are my daily companions.

Daily Prayer

God is my Source.

He is the wind under my wings.

He is the rainbow after the rain.

He is the sun that lights up my path.

He is the air that breathes through me.

He is the star that makes my life shine.

He is the wave that sweeps me off my feet.

He is the moon where my head rests at night.

He is my ALL.

About the Author

Jocelyne F. Lafrenière is an international management consultant, executive coach, corporate trainer, and keynote speaker. She is the President of JFL International Inc., a management consulting, coaching, and training firm.

Jocelyne has served as an advisor to government departments and agencies, United Nations agencies, businesses, and non-profit organizations around the world. She is known for her business acumen and her drive and passion. She is a former partner of KPMG Canada, one of the world's largest professional services firms, where she led the International Development Assistance Services of their Ottawa office.

Jocelyne holds a bachelor's degree in commerce and is a Chartered Professional Accountant and Certified Internal Control Auditor. She is a Certified Professional Success Coach and Neuro-Linguistic Programming Practitioner.

Throughout her career, Jocelyne has actively championed for the empowerment of women, the protection of children, and education. She is the founder of the JFL Foundation, which advances the lives of underprivileged people around the world through education and entrepreneurship. She champions human rights through the JFL Peace Movement. She is a recipient of the Queen Elizabeth II Diamond Jubilee Medal for her significant contribution to the community in Canada and abroad.